How to make fried Rice:

A guide on how make Nigerian fried rice (Recipe)

Wilson Kane

Table of contents

Chapter 1:Introduction

Chapter 2:How to make Nigerian fried Rice

Chapter 3:Steps on how to make fried rice.

Chapter 4:How to make the classic Nigerian fried Rice

Chapter 5: storing and reheating

Chapter 6: Frequently asked questions

Chapter 7:Difference between Nigerian fried rice and Chinese fried rice

Chapter 8:World's best dishes that you should know

Chapter 1:Introduction

Fried rice is a meal of cooked rice that has been stir-fried in a wok or a frying pan and is generally combined with various items such as eggs, vegetables, seafood, or meat. It is commonly eaten by itself or as a complement to another meal. Fried rice is a common component of East Asian, Southeast Asian, and some South Asian cuisines, as well as a traditional national dish of Indonesia. As a handmade meal, fried rice is generally cooked using ingredients left over from previous recipes, resulting in numerous variants. Fried rice evolved during the Sui Dynasty in China and as such all fried rice dishes may trace their roots to Chinese fried rice.

Many versions of fried rice have a distinct list of ingredients. In Greater China, popular variations include Yangzhou fried rice and Hokkien fried rice. Japanese chāhan is considered a Japanese Chinese food, having developed from Chinese fried rice dishes. Korean bokkeum-bap in general is not of Korean Chinese heritage, however, there is a Korean Chinese type of bokkeum-bap. In Southeast Asia, similarly built Indonesian, Malaysian, and Singaporean nasi goreng and Thai Khao phat are popular dishes. In the West, most restaurants catering to vegetarians have devised their versions of fried rice, including egg fried rice. Fried rice is often featured on the menus of American restaurants providing cuisines with no national heritage of the dish. Additionally, the cuisine of various Latin American nations features variants of fried rice, such as Ecuadorian charlatan, Peruvian Arroz chaufa, Cuban Arroz Frito, and Puerto Rican Arroz Hampstead.

Fried rice is a traditional street snack in Asia. In several Asian nations, tiny eateries, street sellers and roving hawkers specialize in offering fried rice. In Indonesian cities, it is usual to locate fried rice street hawkers wandering around the streets with their food cart and stationing it in busy streets or residential neighborhoods. Many Southeast Asian street food booths provide fried rice with a range of optional toppings and side dishes.

Chapter 2:How to make Nigerian fried Rice

INGREDIENTS

Rice: However, Nigerian fried rice is generally cooked using parboiled long grain rice.

To cook meat

1.2-kilogram chicken

1 Thumb sized ginger(diced or minced)\s3 cloves garlic chopped

1 little onion chopped

1 tsp salt

2 knorr chicken cube

1½ tsp curry powder

1 tsp dried thyme or 3 sprigs of fresh thyme

½ cup water\for the rice

3 cups basmati rice Sella basmati or parboiled rice (see note 2) (see note 2)

2 cups meat stock

1 cup water

2 tsp curry powder

1 tsp salt

1 tsp white pepper optional

½ bell pepper\veggies

1 bundle scallions

1 medium carrot\s1 medium green bell pepper

½ cup green peas

¼ cup sweet corn frozen or canned

handful green beans

½ tsp each: salt, garlic powder, curry, thyme
2 tsp white pepper or cayenne pepper
1 chicken cube\soother ingredients
½ cup shrimp boiled and fried see note 1
⅓ cup beef liver cooked, chopped, and fried
3 tbsp vegetable oil
Instructions
In a medium saucepan, prepare beef with the ingredients specified, and boil for 15 -20 minutes. While meat is simmering, prepare your other ingredients. When meat is done, remove meat from stock, fry, and grill to air-fry the meat.
Filter the beef stock, bring liquid back to the saucepan, and add rinsed rice, salt, pepper, curry, and bell pepper pieces. Allow rice to boil until cooked but not entirely soft. Fluff up, turn off the heat, and put aside.
Meanwhile, devein and fried shrimp, and add a sprinkling of salt and pepper to taste. furthermore, boil, dice, and fry liver if used.
In a big wok or skillet, heat vegetable oil, cook veggies beginning with the carrots and green beans, add the other vegetables, and salt, and other spices, and fry for 6-8 minutes.
Add cooked shrimp, liver, rice, and stir fry for approximately 5 minutes then add chopped scallions(spring onions) (spring onions).
Cook fried rice for 5-8 minutes for the ultimate delectable fried rice and serve with coleslaw, fried pork, and fried plantain.

Note 1. Cooking methods for liver:

Cook in boiling water seasoned with salt, seasoning cube. Cook for about 5 minutes.
Remove from water when cooked.
Dice cooked liver into cubes
Heat oil in a pan, and fry liver on low heat for 5-8 minutes. Transfer to a paper towel to drain excess oil.
Note 2. What type of rice works best? Nigerian dishes are usually cooked with long grain parboiled rice. The closest alternative is Sella basmati rice(what I used for this recipe) (what I used for this recipe). You may also use basmati rice or brown rice.
Note 3. Fresh or frozen vegetables? Fresh veggies are usually ideal but you may also use frozen(thawed) if you don't have access to fresh vegetables.

Chapter 3:Steps on how to make fried rice.

Nigerian Fried Rice Recipe

Nigerian Fried Rice is a really easy but tasty meal. This variation depends on a ton of fresh veggies, Beef Liver, and a tiny amount of oil for crisping everything up.

Close-up image of the wonderful Nigerian Fried Rice laden with assorted veggies and beef Liver

The additional cow liver gives the fried Rice a wonderfully rich yet subtle flavor, and this is why it is one of the most popular options in Nigeria. Though you may also use Shrimp or whatever protein you'd like. If you would wish to create vegan fried rice, you may eliminate the Beef liver or Shrimp!

This fried rice is entirely different from the popular Asian Chicken Fried Rice because the depth of the taste in the latter comes from the Soy sauce while the depth of taste of the latter comes from the Curry powder, Thyme, Seasoning cubes, and of course the abundance of vegetables like Carrots, Green beans, Peas, sweet corn, and Onions.

Just like Jollof Rice we enjoy these dinners so much, and we can scarcely do without them at gatherings and festive seasons, and it's a meal you can cook in no time.

Such a simple meal, but the effect it produces in a gathering is rather astonishing! You may find fantastic Rice recipes here.

This dish begins with already parboiled rice, so it makes the entire procedure simpler. If you don't have previously parboiled rice, you may see how to do so here. It's also alright to use day-old rice that has been refrigerated. It is incredibly handy, and the outcome is just as wonderful.

I also cooked this parboiled rice in a little well-seasoned stock so that the Rice may absorb additional flavor. Though it's advised to do this, however, this step may be ignored if you are in a hurry.

Fresh Rice or Leftover Rice?
You may use either freshly cooked rice (parboiled) or leftover cold rice for this dish. If you opt to use freshly cooked rice, make sure you use the proper sort of Rice. I prefer to use the long grain parboiled rice. This sort of Rice is extremely simple to deal with while producing Fried Rice likewise, Jollof Rice since it's firmer and less sticky, consequently, making it very impossible to go wrong when working with it.

Another trick to attaining a decent outcome when cooking this fried rice is to let the newly cooked rice (parboiled) cool slightly before using it. The rice should be cold to the touch before putting it in the pan. If you are short of time, just put the rice on a sheet pan so that the steam can easily escape, or just store the cooked rice inside the fridge for a few minutes.

Finally, it is crucial that you always wash the rice before cooking it. This will assist to eliminate the extra starch on the rice, which may cause the rice to be clumped together.

Other rice dishes you may want to try:
Coconut Fried Rice– Rice fried with broth and coconut milk. Simply delicious!
Easy shrimp pineapple fried rice - Ready in around 30 minutes
Jollof rice - West Africa's favorite rice dish
One-pot chicken with Rice – Another one you need to try
Chicken fried rice - So simple and tasty!
Hearty mushroom rice - Not your typical mushroom Rice
East African Pilau - You will adore this!
Baked Seafood Jambalaya — a variation on the heritage Jambalaya

Notes On How To Make Nigerian Fried Rice:\sIt's alright to add a dash of cayenne pepper if you prefer some heat!
Don't over-boil your Rice before frying it, else, you will end up with sloppy fried rice.
Fried rice is most appreciated when the Vegetables stay crisp, so don't overcook your veggies.

I used mixed vegetables which consist of Carrots, Sweet Peas, Sweet Corn, and Green Beans. However, veggies like sweet bell peppers may also be utilized.

In order to create that wonderful sought crisp, you will need to crank up the heat to high throughout the frying process and stir continually while you allow the rice to cook up.

I added bits of beef liver to my fried Rice. A lot of people like this as well, but if you don't like it you are free to leave it out, you will still enjoy the whole pleasure of the Fried Rice.

When cooking this Fried Rice, it is advisable to use Chicken stock or Turkey stock because of their moderate flavor. The beef stock should be avoided since it might overshadow the flavor of the fried rice.

Here is my extremely easy but tasty approach to cooking my fried Rice. It is incredibly basic, and the end outcome is great. Enjoy!

Chapter 4:How to make the classic Nigerian fried Rice

Nigerian Fried Rice Recipe
Nigerian fried rice is a traditional lunch, supper, and even celebration food in Nigeria. Very easy but excellent recipe. This variation utilizes mixed veggies and Beef liver; you may substitute Shrimp or whatever protein you'd like. You may eliminate the beef liver if you love to create vegan fried rice.
4.78 from 120 votes
Print Pin Rate
Course: Lunch/Dinner
Cuisine: African
Keyword: fried rice, homemade Prep Time: 10 minutes
Cook Time: 15 minutes Total Time: 25 minutes Servings: 5 person Calories: 227kcal Author: Lola Osinkolu
Ingredients
2 cups cooked rice
1/2 cup chicken stock
3 tablespoon oil for frying
1 cup onion diced
1 cup mixed Vegetables Carrots, Sweet Peas, Sweet Corn, and green beans
1/2 tsp thyme
1 teaspoon Curry powder
2 scallions diced
1 chicken stock cube
1 cup beef liver cubed\salt to taste

1/4 teaspoon Cayenne pepper

Instructions
Add the cooked rice to the stock in a medium saucepan
and simmer over medium heat until the water has dried
up.
Preheat the oil in a skillet on medium to high heat, pour
in the onions, and cook for a minute or two; add the
scallions, mixed veggies, thyme, curry powder, salt, and
stock Cube.
Throw in the beef liver and rice — Stir-fry for roughly 3
to 5 minutes on high heat.
Take it off the heat and serve.
Notes\sThe white rice should be cooked soft but still firm
to bite (as you cook your pasta al-dente) (like you cook
your pasta al-dente). Overcooking the rice can result in
soggy fried rice.
Fried rice is most appreciated when the Vegetables stay
crisp, so don't overcook your veggies.
You need to raise the heat and stir regularly to acquire
that wonderful sought crisp while cooking.

Chapter 5: storing and reheating

Nigerian fried Rice and other rice recipes filled with veggies may go bad rapidly if not cooked and kept correctly.

Well-cooked fried rice may be prepared up to 3 days ahead and kept in the refrigerator or frozen for up to a month.

To guarantee the rice doesn't go bad. Make sure no liquid remains while stir-frying the veggies.

Reheating fried rice lets you enjoy the rice as if it was just made. How you reheat your rice will rely on how it was kept in the very first instance.

If the rice was frozen, let it thaw in the refrigerator overnight then reheat in the microwave or stovetop (using a broad pan) until all moisture from condensation is absorbed this way you don't have to eat soggy rice.

If it was in the refrigerator, warming in the microwave in a covered microwave-safe dish until the meal is cooked through works great. I don't like to add water to fried rice while reheating it.

If you are afraid that the rice might be dry, add a few drops of water or broth. However, I have noticed that the covered dish helps produce some steam and moisture in the rice preventing it from drying out.

Chapter 6: Frequently asked questions

What are the major components of fried rice?

This depends on the sort of fried rice you are creating. For Nigerian fried rice, the basic components are raw rice, beef stock, seasoning, cooking oil, and mixed vegetables whereas for Asian style fried rice, you need to cook white rice, eggs, oil, veggies, and soy sauce.

Do you cook the rice before you fry it?

To create fried rice you need a cooked rice. The rice is either a day-old white rice or boiled in beef stock before mixing with stir-fried veggies.

WHAT IS NIGERIAN FRIED RICE?
Nigerian fried rice is a rice meal that's created with meats, mixed vegetables (carrots, peas, sweet corn, green beans), and seasonings. Like jollof rice, It is a typical component at parties. What makes this dish genuine is the use of liver as the protein of choice.

Chapter 7:Difference between Nigerian fried rice and Chinese fried rice

Nigerian Fried Rice and Asian fried rice have certain parallels and distinctions which I will be detailing below. I have included an infographic you may want to share with your relatives and friends.

Differences:

Nigerian fried rice uses rice cooked in meat stock while Chinese fried rice uses cool white rice which is usually a day old.
Chinese Fried rice uses eggs (scrambled) as part of its ingredients while African fried rice doesn't use eggs.
Nigerian fried rice derives its color from curry while the other gets its color from soy sauce or oyster sauce.

Similarities: Both recipes are made with Rice, veggies, some oil with or without some form of animal protein.

Chapter 8: World's best dishes that you should know

Rice is one of the most eaten foods in the world. This grain was so essential throughout history that it even functioned as a payment currency in the days of feudal Japan (the koku was the quantity required to feed a person for a year) (the koku was the amount needed to feed a person for a year). Another example is rice flinging at weddings, a ritual that developed in China where rice is a symbol of success and plenty.

Its appeal may be explained by the range of types (there are more than 40 thousand kinds of rice) and techniques of preparation that can allow it to be loose, brothy, or sticky. Also, rice is highly adaptable, being served as a traditional side, a delectable main meal, and even as a dessert.

Check out next some of the most renowned rice recipes in the world:

- Galinhada
- Biryani\sPilaf
- Paella
- Arroz Al Horno
- Arroz de Polvo
- Nasi Lemak
- Nasi Goreng
- Sushi
- Bibimbap

- Pad Kra Pao\sRisotto
- Jambalaya
- Jollof Rice\Arroz Chaufa

Galinhada

Galinhada is one of the most recognized comfort dishes in Brazil. The primary elements of this great Sunday supper are rice, chicken, and spices (parsley, green onions, turmeric, and cumin) with many modifications depending on the location.

The most crucial thing about the Galinhada dish is to cook the rice simultaneously with the chicken. It's excellent and simple to cook, after all, you'll only need to wash one pan.

Biryani\Biryani is one of the most traditional cuisines in India and its origin is still a topic of controversy. Traditional Biryani is cooked using Basmati rice, meats (most usually chicken or lamb), and numerous spices like black pepper, cumin, saffron, cardamom, mint, ginger, nutmeg, and bay leaf.

Other components that may be used, depending on the location, include potatoes, almonds, dried fruits, rose water, and yogurt. Biryani is often eaten in festivities like weddings and on Eid (the final day of Ramadan) and has two traditional techniques of cooking known as Kacchi and Pakki.

biryani rice with mutton, one of the most renowned rice dishes in the world

Pilaf
Originating in the Middle East, the name Pilaf refers to
the technique of cooking rice (or other cereals such as
quinoa and amaranth) that leaves the grains very loose.
In the recipe, the rice is sautéed with oil or ghee butter,
onion, and various spices (eg: cinnamon, cardamom,
cumin, star anise) before the addition of vegetable broth,
which makes the rice aromatic and tasty.

Paella\sPaella is undoubtedly one of the most popular
rice dishes in the West. Although it is fairly common to
see paellas cooked with seafood, these components are
not part of the traditional recipe (Paella Valenciana),
which contains bomba-type rice, chicken, rabbit meat,
snails, tomatoes, saffron, rosemary, garrofón (a sort of
big white bean) and Herradura (similar to green bean)
(similar to green bean). Paella with seafood is known as
Paella Marinera.

The word paella originally relates to the pan used to
create the cuisine, distinguished by being big, spherical,
and having handles.

Arroz Al Horno
In addition to the famous Paella, the city of Valencia
boasts Arroz Al Horno as another distinctive cuisine. In
this recipe, the rice is first sautéed, then chicken broth is

added and the meal is completed in the oven in a clay pot or ceramic dish, ideally circular.

Arroz al Horno is cooked using bomba-type rice (short grain), pig (ribs and bacon), Spanish blood sausage, potatoes, tomatoes, garlic, saffron, paprika, and chickpeas.

Arroz de Polvo
Arroz de Polvo (octopus rice) is a highly popular rice dish in Portuguese cuisine. The meal is created using Carolina-type rice (long grain), often used in the "Malandrino" style of preparations, a Portuguese name for the more brothy dishes.

In this dish, rice is cooked in the same broth used to boil the octopus, which assures extra flavor. It also needs olive oil, tomatoes, white wine, as well as numerous spices like onions, garlic, bay leaves, black pepper, and coriander.

Nasi Lemak
Among so many traditional Malaysian dishes, Nasi Lemak is regarded as the iconic dish of Malay cuisine. Nasi means rice and Lemak may be interpreted as rich or delectable. Rice (jasmine or other long-grain) is boiled in water with coconut milk, pandan leaves (a leaf that has a similar aroma to vanilla), and spices.

Rice is traditionally served with Sambal (hot sauce with shrimp paste), fried dry anchovies, cucumber, and toasted peanuts. As a protein supplement, you may add egg, tofu, or fried chicken.

Nasi Goreng
Nasi Goreng is one of the most popular foods in Indonesia and means fried rice. The rice is mixed with the sweet Kecap Manis sauce, made with soy sauce, sugar, pepper, ginger, kaffir lime leaves, and tamarind juice. The dish can be added with vegetables, and meat and served with fried egg and krupuk (a kind of chips made with starch).

Sushi Icon of Japanese cuisine, sushi is considered to be any preparation made with short-grain cooked rice (this type of rice has a high starch content, which makes the grains stick together), vinegar, sugar, and salt.

There are several types of sushi, such as Makizushi (one of the most famous, where the dumpling is wrapped in a sheet of dried seaweed and can have different fillings such as vegetables, omelet, and raw fish) and Nigiri (dumpling covered by a slice that can be raw fish, octopus, shrimp or egg).

Bibimbap

Bibimbap is one of the best-known dishes in Korean cuisine and is considered the national dish of the country.

This delicacy is made with glutinous rice, a variety of vegetables (eg: spinach, bean sprouts, carrots, zucchini), shiitake mushroom, stripped meat (usually beef), egg, and a red pepper paste, the gochujang. When served in a very hot stone pot (called Dolsot) it is called Dolsot Bibimbap.

Pad Kra Pao
In Thai, Pad means fried and Kra Pao is the name given to the herb known as Thai Basil, one of the main ingredients of this recipe. The rice used is jasmine (long grain), fried with garlic, Thai basil, bird's eye pepper (also known as Thai pepper), and protein of choice (chicken, pork, beef, seafood, or tofu). It is usually served with a fried egg on top.

Risotto
This list would not be complete if we did not mention Risotto, a dish that was invented in the Italian region of Lombardy. To make risotto, the rice is sautéed and then slowly cooked in broth (from vegetables or meat) (from vegetables or meat). There are numerous risotto recipes, most of which, like many Italian dishes, harmonize very well with wines.

One of the main characteristics of the risotto is its creaminess, so you should use rice that releases starch when cooked, such as arbóreo, carnaroli, and viable nano, which are the most used types.

Jambalaya\sJambalaya is a rice dish originating in the city of New Orleans (USA) (USA). Made with rice and traditionally chicken or pork meat, smoked sausage, and seafood like shrimp. There are two versions of Jambalaya, Cajun and Creole. The difference between the two lies in the technique of preparation and also in some of the components, such as the inclusion of tomatoes in the Creole version.

By the way, Cajun flavor is regarded as one of the best seasonings in the world and may be used in many other dishes.

Jollof Rice
Jollof Rice is a rice meal that is extremely famous in West African nations, notably in Nigeria and Ghana, who ceaselessly fight who makes the greatest Jollof, even though they were not the founders of the highly renowned delicacy, origin assigned to the Wolof people of Senegal and Gambia.

Well, tale aside, in the Jollof dish, rice is boiled in a broth prepared with tomatoes, peppers, onions, and red pepper (it is popular to add Scotch Bonnet pepper,

which provides an intensity similar to Habanero pepper),
all beaten. Subsequently, additional spices are added to
it such as curry powder, bay leaf, and thyme. A superb
rice dish with dramatic and spicy tastes.

Arroz Chaufa
Chaufa Rice is a Peruvian variant of Chinese fried rice
— the meal is part of Chifa cuisine, established by
Chinese immigrants who altered their recipes with
Peruvian ingredients.

This recipe is a fantastic way to utilize leftover cooked
rice, fried in a Wok pan with soy sauce, sesame oil,
garlic, onion, egg, chives, peppers, and chopped meat
(beef, hog, or chicken) or shrimp.

.

www.ingramcontent.com/pod-product-compliance
Lightning Source LLC
Chambersburg PA
CBHW071258140726

47996CB00007B/2892